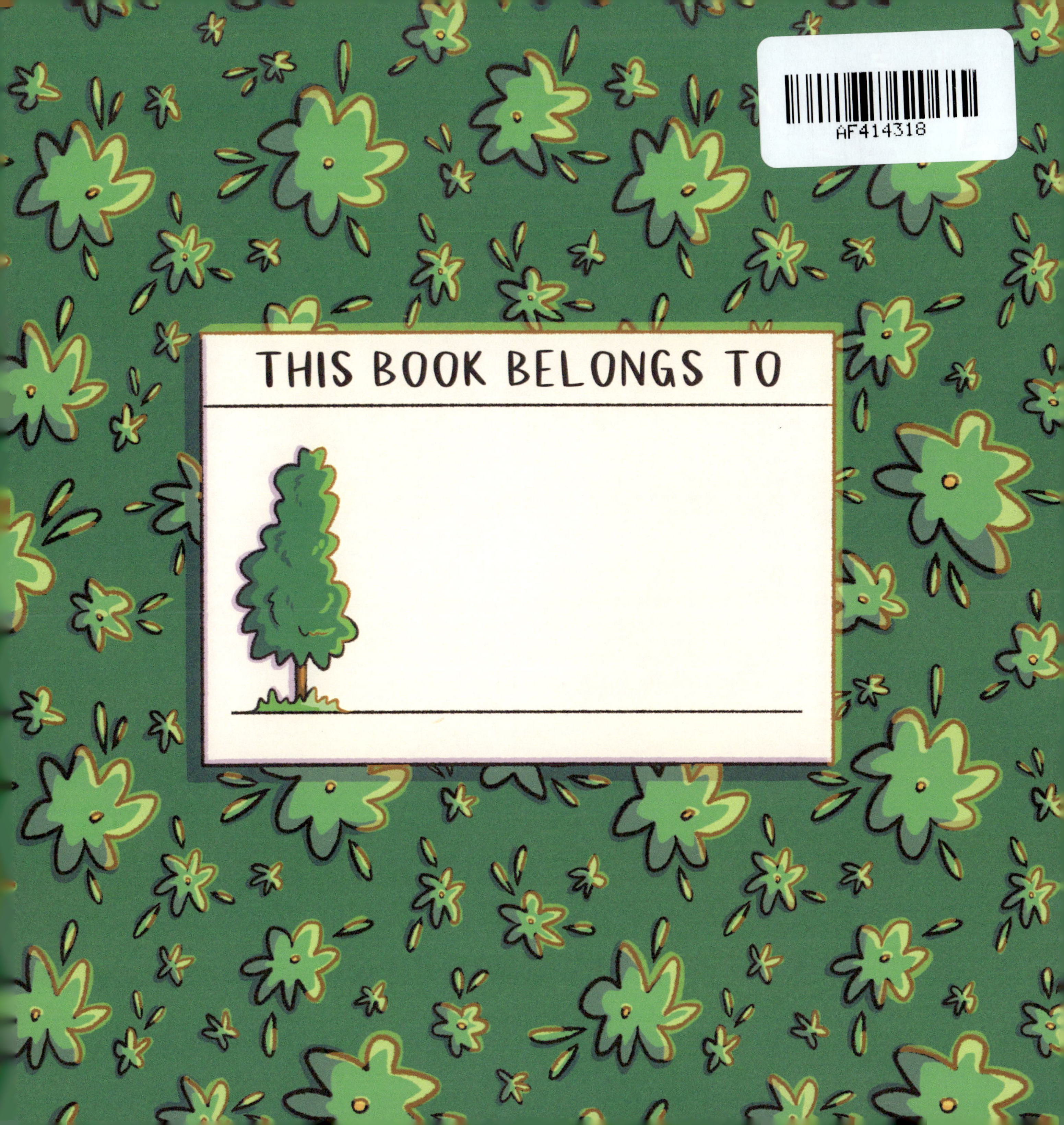

AF414318
THIS BOOK BELONGS TO

FIRE
IN THE
FOREST

Written by MACIE MOORE
Illustrated by RAHAT MOTIWALLA

Fires can be scary
when used the wrong way

They can burn and scorch
and turn the sky grey

Fires can make big flames
and little ones too

But fires can be important
to both me and you

Fires can keep us warm
on cold chilly nights

They can help us celebrate
or make tasty delights

Out in the forest
fires can be bad

But sometimes little flaming fires
can make the forest glad

As they rumble and tumble
through the forest land

Fires can help grow the forest
better than humans had planned

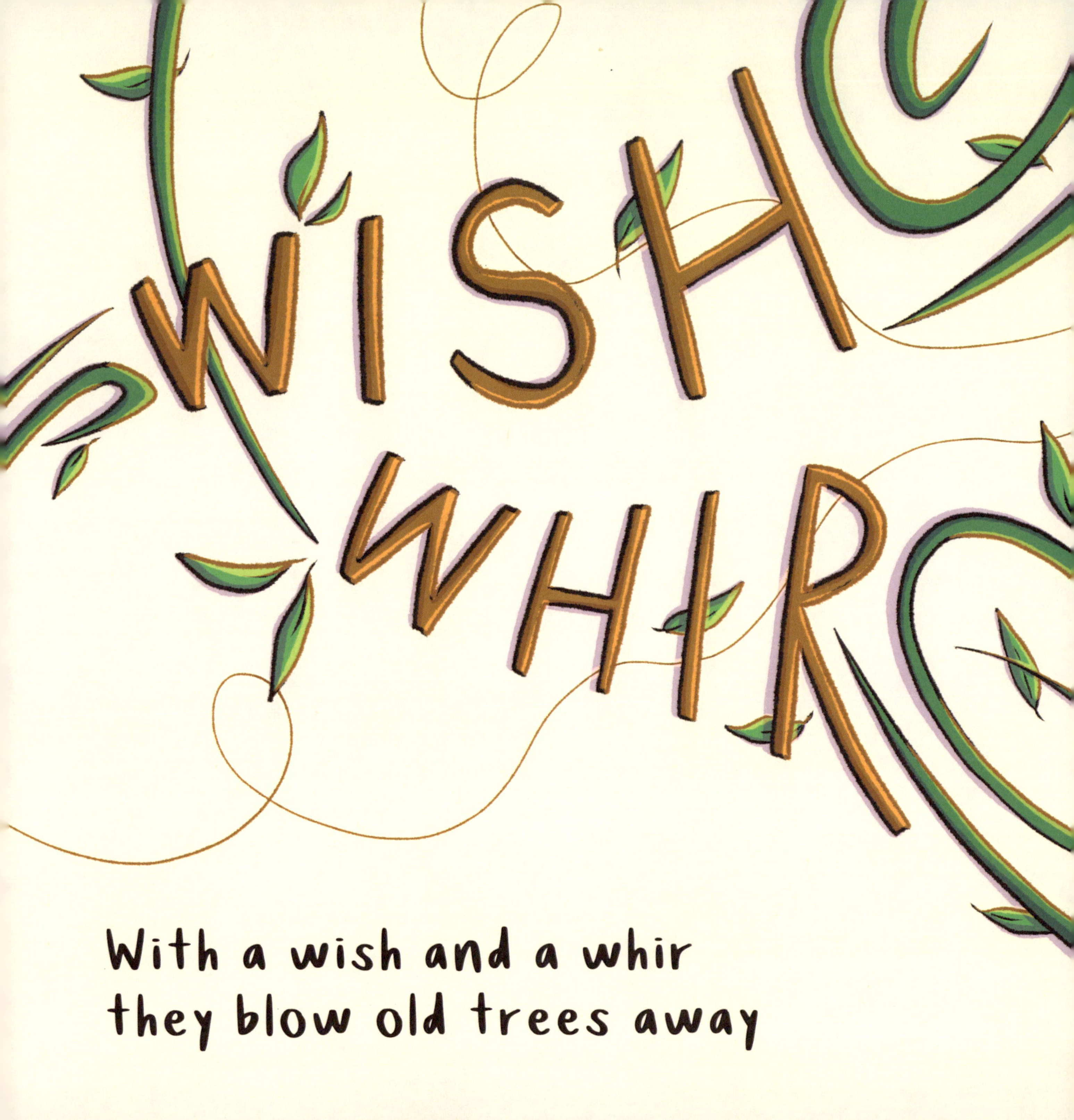

With a wish and a whir
they blow old trees away

Making room for new trees
to come out and play

As they spark and glow
they clean the forest floor 

Even making sure
that future fires don't roar

Yes, fires can be helpful
when the flames don't get too big

It's important to remember
the life that they give

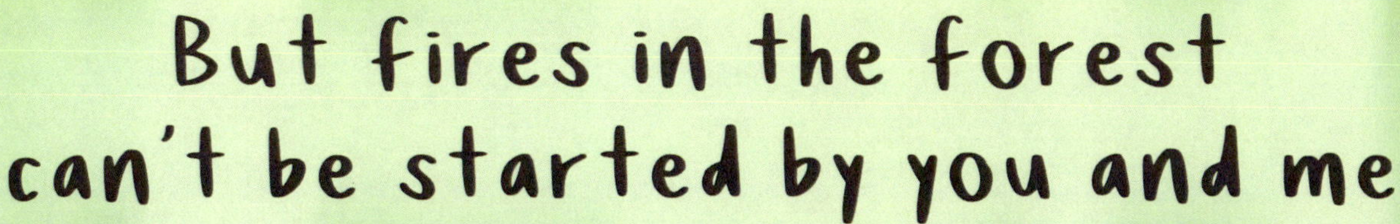

But fires in the forest
can't be started by you and me

They need a professional
to guide them you see

Special people
in special safe suits

Walk through the forest
in their fireproof boots

Using tools and their training
with water they spray

Doing their best
to keep big fires away

Always remember
fire isn't a toy

We should never start fires
it won't bring us joy

Caution!

Only trust an adult
to handle the flame

Because playing with fire
isn't a game

Yes, fires are dangerous
they can hurt you and me

But when used the right way
they can help save the trees

Macie
Rahat
Macie and Rahat have teamed up to create "Fire in the Forest", their debut picture book. Together, they hope to raise awareness about the benefits of prescribed burns, land management, and ecological conservation.